The Measure of a Woman
The Details of Her Soul

The Measure of a Woman

OTHER BOOKS BY ONEDIA N. GAGE

As We Grow Together Daily Devotional for Expectant Couples

As We Grow Together Prayer Journal for Expectant Couples

The Blue Print: Poetry for the Soul

In Purple Ink: Poetry for the Spirit

Living An Authentic Life

On This Journey Daily Devotional for Young People

On This Journey Prayer Journal for Young People

Promises, Promises

Yielded and Submitted: A Woman's Journey of a Life Dedicated to God

The Measure of a Woman
The Details of Her Soul

Onedia N. Gage

Purple Ink, Inc Press
Houston

The Measure of a Woman
The Details of Her Soul

All Rights Reserved © 2009 Onedia N. Gage

No part of this of book may be reproduced or transmitted in
Any form or by any means, graphic, electronic, or mechanical,
Including photocopying, recording, taping, or by any
Information storage or retrieval system, without the
Permission in writing from the publisher.

Purple Ink, Inc. Press

For Information address:
Purple Ink, Inc
P. O. Box 27242
Houston, TX 77227
www.purpleink.net

ISBN: 978-0-9801002-4-2

Printed in United States

The Details of Her Soul

For I say, through the grace given unto me, to every that is among you, not to think of himself more highly than he ought to think; but to think soberly, according as God has dealt to every man the measure of faith.

Romans 12:3 KJV

I will praise thee; for I am fearfully and wonderfully made: marvelous are thy works; and that my soul knoweth right well.

Psalm 139:14 KJV

So when they continued asking him, he lifted up himself, and said unto them, "He that is without sin among you, let him cast the first stone at her."

John 8:7 KJV

DEDICATION

To the Women whose
Testimony is within these
Pages

May this poetry inspire you
To address your issues
And
Find your truest self

TABLE OF CONTENTS

The Dimension of the Woman
The Naked Eye	19
The Maintenance of a Woman	21
The Woman in the Photo	22
What's Missing From the Picture	23
A Fragile Heart	24
Heart Broken	25
Defensive Player of the Year	26
The Perfect Ten	27
The Perfect Ten to My Heart	28
The Woman of Your Dreams	29
Eyes Don't Lie	30
Just Talk to Me	31
Secrets	32
Everything She's Not	33
A Woman of Few Words	34
My Love Will Overwhelm You	35
Exception to the Rules	36
Get Out of the Truck	38
No Approval Required	40
Crystal Clear	41
Not Now But Someday	42
Diva, How Are You?	43
Storm	44

The Dynamic of the Woman
Oops, I Did It Again	51
A Spectacular Failure	52
Your Eyes . . . But	53
Separate Agendas	54
From One Drop to a Flood	55
Because Leftovers Won't Do	56
The Definition of a Little While	57
A Fragile Marriage	58
Covenant Under Scrutiny	60
We Exhausted the Possibilities	61
With a Hardened Heart	62
Endings	63
Is This A Test of Will	64
No Promises Required	65
On Your Terms	66
His/Hers	67
Expect Some Consequences	68
The Starting Five	69
Walked Away	70
Hide and Seek	71
Love Letter	72
San Antonio, Texas	73
Conditional Love	74

The Dreams of the Woman

The First Lady	81
Beautiful Chemistry	82
Love Ethic	83
Great Music	84
The Truth Is	85
Reminded	86
It's You I Crave	87
Unforgiving Rules	88
Pouring Rains	89
A Penny for Your Thoughts	90
A Time to Love	91
Your Transparency	92
The Tension	93
Dangerous	94
Because Of . . . You	95
Between the Drops	96
Intimate Distance	97
The Look Said It All	98
Hand Over the Trophy	99
Lovers Don't Quarrel	101
In the Presence of the Present	102
You Started It	103
Instant Love	104
The State of the Relationship Address	105
The Tester Bottle	106
Truer Still	107
Looking Around for Love	108
Timing Is Everything	109
Good Eyes	110
Across The Spectrum	111
My Safe Place	112
In	113
The Measure of a Woman	115

THE MEASURE OF A WOMAN

THE DETAILS OF HER SOUL

Gage's definition of the Measure of a Woman:

The fullness of that woman from head to heart to toes. This definition includes her work, her family and her love. This Measure includes the depth, breadth, height, and width of her love capacity and all other characteristics.

This encompasses the resilience of a woman.

This measure also explains why she is defined as a woman. Her profound acts and wisdom and the love she experiences which introduces the hurts she encounters but eventually endures.

Experience The Measure of a Woman.

The Dimension Of the Woman

THE DIMENSION OF THE WOMAN

di·men·sion

[di-**men**-sh*uh* n, dahy-]

a. measurement in length, width, and thickness.
b. scope; importance: *the dimensions of a problem.*

THE NAKED EYE

To the naked eye
    I look great
    My hair—each one in place
    My nails—just right
    My toes—perfectly polished

To the naked eye
    I'm hard and direct
    Abrasive and crass
    Tacky and unprofessional, to some
    Yet professional and effective, to others
    HIGH MAINTENANCE

To the naked eye
    Statements profound
    Poetic words
    Successful endeavors
    Aggressive career path
    Accomplishments abound

To the naked eye
    Happy
    Content
    Satisfied
    Well-connected
    Charismatic, even

To the naked eye
    Handful
    Perfectionist

But to the heart's eye
    I'm sensitive and
    Caring
    Loving
    Lovable
    Kind

To the heart's eye
    Guarded
    Controlled
    Thoughtful
    Pensive
    Cautious

To the heart's eye
    Passionate
    Romantic
    Hopelessly so

Profoundly poetic
Shy

To the heart's eye
    I'm curious
    Educated
    Friendly
    Adventuresome
    Unknown

Use the Heart's Eye
    To see the authentic me
    To know the rich me
    To seek the spiritual me
    To unlock the mysteries
    To love me

THE MAINTENANCE OF A WOMAN

Hair pressed, weaved, chi'ed, permed, curled
Nails solar, gel, airbrushed, clipped, painted
Feet rubbed, scrubbed, mud-dipped, polished
Eyebrows plucked, waxed, threaded, snipped
That's all she needs
And some regular tune-ups
Not so much
That's not all at all

Tap her soul
Access her quietness
Seek her gentleness
Maintenance of a woman
Requires more than spa time
She requires your time
Your time alone
No television
No games
Just the two of you
Intently focused on her
That's not all though

Look into her eyes
Ask her what she is thinking
Ask her how she feels
And her needs
Her knowledge
What is her love language
You'll never know until you inquire
What is her love language
Likes and dislikes
Baths and showers
Minor I know
But essential indeed
Not all though

Listen to her words
Listen for the feelings behind the words
Dig deep within
For the jewel
Access that jewel—
The accessories gifted you
A real woman
Requires maintenance
Not just an oil change
High maintenance
Maintenance well worth it
If you deserve her, if only glimpses of her
Then maintain that woman.

THE WOMAN IN THE PHOTO

She's pretty
       . . . but what's behind her eyes
She's glamorous
       . . . but what's on her mind
She has diva attitude and everything
       . . . but what makes her happy, angry and sad
She's smiling
       . . . but is she really
She's almost laughing
       . . . but is it authentic
She appears happy
       . . . but what does she need

The woman in the photo
Investigate her
Probe her for the details
Pay attention to the subtleties
Precise are her moves
Poised are her moods

Is that vision of beauty
       Hiding hurt
       Harboring anger
       Healing from harm
Take note of the woman in the photo
Each detail of her being
Test for her authenticity

The woman in the photo
Requires your attention
Requests your affection
Resigns for love
Recognizes your fear
Relinquishes her power
Retaliates from hate
Responds with care
Relies on honesty
Relishes in peace

The woman in the photo
       Is real
       Is a reality
       Is a dream realized

The Woman in the Photo.

WHAT'S MISSING FROM THE PICTURE

That blank stare said it all
Something is missing from the picture

Matching outfits	present
Professional photographer	present
Props	present
Flawless skin	present
2.2 kids	present
Authentic smile	
Authentic smile	
Authentic smile	no answer

How long has that been missing
Was it missing from the last photographic session
When did it disappear
What happened to the authentic smile
We need that back
Where can we retrieve the smile
Can we buy the authentic smile back
Can we massage it back to the top of her expression
Can we hug it back into existence
Can we pray it back to her complexion
Can we talk and laugh to return the authentic smile

The authentic smile could return
Can you love her authentic smile back to her face
It is missing but it almost wasn't missed

A Fragile Heart

Such passion
So much strength
A stickler for details
This warm heart
Endures conditional love
Encounters criticism
Missing comfort
Denied care

Eager to please
Enjoys long talks
Welcomes long walks
Yearns for unconditional love

High spirited
Highly competitive
High maintenance
Highly spiritual

Nurture it
Through time,
Love and tenderness
Cherish it's spirit
Touch the boundaries

Massage the heart with kind words
And significant deeds
And long baths.

A Fragile Heart

HEART BROKEN

Did you hear her heart break?
Can you hear her irregular heart beat?
The irregular heart beat results from brokenness.

Did you see her heart break?
Can you see her heart break?
The breaking heart is breaking under
      Your very stare.

Did you feel her heart break?
Can you feel her heart break?
Her heart breaks under your very touch.

Did you understand her heart break?
Did you know that her heart was breaking?
Were you sensitive to her pain?
Were you there when her heart was broken?

Did you plan on helping her heart heal?
Did you plan on wiping her tears?
Did you plan on soothing her aches?

Pay attention to her details.
She is suffering from heart break.

DEFENSIVE PLAYER OF THE YEAR

She inches away with such class
Same demeanor
Same smile
Same words
Fewer of them, though

Daily visits transition
To weekly meetings
To chance sightings
Now you are working your way onto her agenda
      —not the reverse

Fort Knox is under security realignment
Password changes
New admittance qualifications
Lengthened waiting periods

Conversations lightened into
Virtual non-existence

Transparency transitions to opaque
Fort Knox added the distance detail
Due to last security breach
All clear communication that:
      Her hurt overwhelmed her
      Her needs neglected
      Her heart broken
      Her body sometimes betrays her
      Her mind has resumed the helm of control

The defensive player of the year
Sent a message to the team
Fort Knox is fully operational
Security level: Orange

Defensive player of the year
Protected
Guarded
Strong
Powerful
Elusive
Mysterious
Alluring
Proud
Yet unavailable
Defense requires focus
Defensive Player of the Year

THE PERFECT TEN

Ten to my heart
A perfect ten exists
In search of the perfect ten
This ten encompasses my heart
This ten occupies my soul
This ten motivates my spirit

Ten is perfect
Ten is consistent
Ten creates comfort
Ten seeks a fertile heart
Ten covers the needs of a soul

The Perfect Ten accesses my emotional wellness
The Perfect Ten stimulates intimacy
The Perfect Ten discovers depths
The Perfect Ten exists
The Perfect Ten loves
The Perfect Ten defines me

THE PERFECT TEN TO MY HEART

Perfection exists somewhere
But not in we
Lacking in the perfect ten
    No kindness
    No care
    No concern
    No attention
    No conversation
    No intimacy
    No time
    No investment
    No maintenance
    Last

The Perfect Ten to my heart
    Second, not last
    Investment
    Time
    Intimacy
    Conversation
    Attention
    Concern
    Listening
    Respect
    Love
    Intimacy

Just want to have The Perfect Ten
In search of The Perfect Ten
The Perfect Ten communicates
Love in fascinating ways
The Perfect Ten motivates care
The Perfect Ten stimulates profound passion

Just need The Perfect Ten

THE WOMAN OF YOUR DREAMS

Magnet
Magnetic
Magnetism at it's finest
Overwhelming attraction
Is she real?
Is she your reality?
Is she realistic?

Was she your dream?
In your dreams?
Which one of your wildest dreams?
Are you still dreaming?

Or did she just pour cold water on you?
Did she cause your "unstable" life to be still for just over a moment?
Why such attraction?
Why this attraction?
Why more than any other?

She meet your criteria?
She meet your needs?
She settle your fears?
She dry your tears?
She listen to your worries?
She love you on your terms?

Do you love her?
Will you always?
The romance started with a vision of a dream
She melted your heart with her first words
She finishes your sentences
She reads your mind
She protects your heart

She is indeed the woman of your dreams

So why did you walk away?
Without so much as a goodbye?

EYES DON'T LIE

They tell it all
The eyes have it
They share the dynamics
Of the inner workings
The secrets
The joy
The hurt
The wonder
The majic
They share the questions
The eyes tell it all
They reach the soul of another
Requesting the intimacy
Requiring the relationship
Eyes tell the truth
The <u>whole</u> story
Nothing but the truth
So help the eyes
The depth of the eye yet to be
        Measurable
Actual depth—yes
Proverbially—no
Emotionally—not even close
Eyes respond to the scene first
They respond to the damage first
The eyes' assessment is the truest assessment
Get the mouth to respond
        In real time
According to the Eye's assessment
Then and only then will you know the truth
The mind tailors the eyes' assessment
For proper presentation
Often neglecting the original context
Or content
Or conviction
The mind refines the response
To disguise the hurt the eyes witnessed
To shield the harm the eyes endure
To protect the storm the eyes foretell
When the heart tells the mouth to
Communicate what the eyes experienced . . .
Eyes don't lie
Eyes respond to the heart's response
Eyes don't lie

Just Talk to Me

Premium conversation
Night time
Day time
Anytime
Just talk
Weather
Groceries
Excitement
Just talk
My feelings
My thoughts
My needs
Just talk
Just talk to me
Just ask me
Compliments
Just sentences
Your feelings
Your needs
Your thoughts
Focused conversation
Phone
Face to face
Email
Telegram
Just talk to me
Is conversation so hard to have?
Premiere conversation
Tired
Sleepy
Awake
Alert
TALK TO ME!
JUST TALK TO ME!

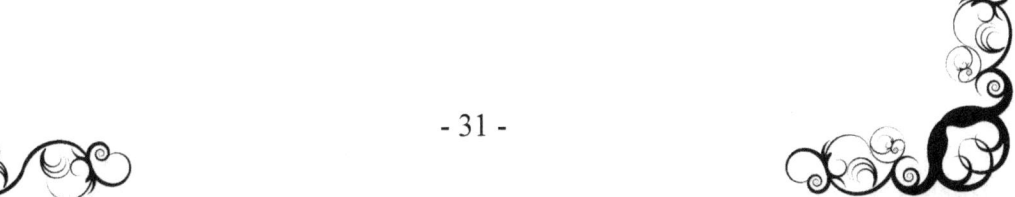

SECRETS

Don't read my secrets

Don't let me keep them to myself

'Cause if I keep them
That translates
Into little communication with you

If we aren't talking
Then we probably
Aren't making love

It's hard to be in love with
And not make love

Do you get my point?

Never keeping secrets

Start talking
Start listening
Start remembering
Start delivering on your promises

EVERYTHING SHE'S NOT

Nagging
Procrastinating
Moaning
Can't get a little peace

Difference is
Innovative
Creative
Wise
Independent

Problem is
Intimidating
Too independent

Two extremes
Too extremes

Considerate
Charismatic
Compassionate
Caring
Confident

Quite opposite
Confined
Confused
Conflict-driven

She ignites the very passion
You try to conceal

She stirs the brewing anger
Which borders on insanity
From today's frustration

Love me for everything I am
Love me for everything she is not

A Woman of Few Words

Disbelief will elude you
Leading you to believe
I was kidding
When I said that
I say it once
Whatever it is
Once it is said
I'm done
No extra explanation
No hidden message
No additional explicative's
No side bar
Direct
Concise
Specific
Words, once delivered
Not to be recovered
These few words
Cherished, appreciated
Respected, remembered
Understood
Misunderstood
Her words are few
Important
Thought-provoking
Emotional stimuli

The blue print to reach her soul:
      Your destination

MY LOVE WILL OVERWHELM YOU

My love will overwhelm

Let my love encompass you
                Pour over you
                Drench you with my passion and prowess

And when I overwhelm
Don't scare
Don't fright
Don't run

It's easier over time
The longer you know me
        —the more you want my love to envelope you

This kind of love is hard to come by
Hard to achieve that level
Harder to maintain
Hardest to return

Be honest
You enjoy those moments
When you race home so that you
Can meet my embrace at the door
You know that you missed me all day
You want to need me
Let my love overwhelm you
Intoxicating love
Drunk love
Deeply satisfying love
Inviting love
That old kind of love
Where lifetime lovers were common

My love will overwhelm you
When it does
        Relax
        Bask
        Enjoy
        Breathe
        Dream
        Live
        Love

An Overwhelming Love

EXCEPTION TO THE RULES

Put the rule book down
That will not work
I am the exception to the rules
Why does the rule book even exist
What did you intend to accomplish with "the rules"

Yes I'm spoiled
But so are you
I know because I did the spoiling

Yes I have high expectations
But so do you
I know because I put them there

Yes I'm high maintenance
But so are you
I know because I set the schedule

Yes I'm a diva
But you like it
I know because I see you smile when I pout

Yes I'm demanding
But you tolerate those demands
Because you are demanding too

So how effective are those rules?

What you won't let her do
You invite me to indulge
Where you don't let her linger
You invite me to relax within
When you shut down
You invite me to stay

These rules designed to protect your heart
Released for my heart to join yours

These rules destined to guard your spirit
Relinquished to seek mine

Those rules determined to prevent the meeting of our bodies
Reversed the security mechanism to unite
An explosive and powerful passion between
Two reconciled lovers

The rules declared to keep your mind preoccupied
Relied too heavily on the wrong occupation
And the truest of passions met to revive

The love they once made

Oh the rules—
In place for great intentions
Designed to spark a reaction
Designed to start a conversation
Deliberately distributed to discourage the foolishness

But I am the exception to the rule
—all of them—
I don't need the rules to respect you
I don't need the rules to communicate with you
I don't need the rules to love you

I made those rules
        —the rules exist because of me.

I established the standard

I am the exception!

GET OUT OF THE TRUCK

Missed a great love
Wasted time
Ignore your mind
Grab the door handle
Get out of the truck

You love that man
Go to him
You cooked for him
You bathed him
Get out of the truck

You yearn for him
You miss him
You sought him
You need him
Get out of the truck

Your fear stopped you
Your responsibilities stumped you
Your idiosyncrasies
Your inadequacies
Get out of the truck

When your memories of him flood your heart
When your memory of your time with him
        Completely overtake your mind
When your heart aches for him
When you anticipate his arrival
Get out of the truck

Real love
True love
Hard to find
Hard to keep
Get out of the truck

Realize real love
Recognize true love
Participate in awesome love
Contribute to authentic love
Get out of the truck

Go to him—in spite on sacrifice
Love him completely—in spite of the distance
Give him yourself decisively—because of your heart
Receive him deeply—because of his
Get out of the truck

You could've spent wonderful years of love with him
You spent days dreaming about
You spent hours wondering where he was
You spent precious moments you cannot recover wanting him
But you didn't get out of the truck.

Safe versus sensitive
Known versus unknown
Stable versus sacrificial
Profound versus perfunctory
Get out of the truck

NO APPROVAL REQUIRED

I don't recall saying that
I was auditioning
For your heart or
Your time
So what exactly gave you that impression?

I am sure that you misunderstood
That my interest involved
Your approval of ME.
The ME that you see and the
ME which hides behind
My outspoken and outlandish and my boisterous
Representative
Were not seeking your approval

I am not subject to your approval
I am not in need of your seal of "ok"
I do not need your conditions
Or your conditional responsiveness

I don't recall indicating that I needed approval
To pursue my heart's desire
Not even if it's you I pursue
Remember that it's you who I like
But need I do not
I am not requesting to be "fixed"
Or "solved"
Or "resolved" like conflict

I am a whole person
—a whole woman
—a whole bunch of woman
A woman whose presence is clever
A woman whose poise is classic
A woman whose passion is climatic
A woman whose pace is challenging
A woman whose position is choosy
A woman whose positivity is charming

This woman defines your approval
In fact maybe she should decline her desire because
If you think she needs your approval
Then you are not the one
Your approval is not required
For the uniquely, fabulous, intelligent, outstanding, over-achiever

But thanks for the offer of your approval

CRYSTAL CLEAR

I believe in fairy tales
I like silly songs and
Love songs
I fall in love because of spent time
I like my feet massaged
I like my hair teased by your hand
I like to feed you grapes while on your back
I like to be whispered to relentlessly
I like ice
My love for strawberries is misunderstood
I laugh at silly stuff
I want to be disturbed in my sleep
Your conversation is my oxygen
I don't like to be without you
I like to read the Sunday paper on Saturday
I sleep late, at least I did
I bathe with lots of bubbles and sugar scrub
Riesling is my favorite wine
I think of you more and more
Can you keep my secrets?
Purple is my absolute favorite color
Let's be clear
I love you
Can you keep your word?
Can you love me?
Please invite me to dance
Please invite me to make love to you.
Say yes when I ask.

NOT NOW BUT SOMEDAY

I haven't given up on love
But I have given up on loving you

I haven't stopped loving
But I stopped loving you

I haven't stopped believing in relationships
But I have stopped believing in this relationship

I haven't given up on life happily ever after
But I have redefined happy and after

I know that it's hard to address this issue
But I know that my hurt will heal
And my pain won't last always

I am certain I will love again.
There is someone for me that will love me unconditionally and completely.
There is someone who I will love, respect, admire and adore.

There is someone who I can share the rest of my life with that will understand my Idiosyncrasies and care that they even exist.

DIVA, HOW ARE YOU?

I looked into your eyes the other day and I didn't like what I saw.
I hadn't looked into your deep, intellectual eyes in awhile,
So when I did, I was surprised that I saw hurt and pain and loneliness.

So Diva, what's wrong? What are we going to do?
I can't afford for you to smile into a slump or a lull or a real depression.
I can't afford for you to take an emotional hiatus or even a break.

So Diva, what can I do to help you?
Do we need to come and clean your house?
Or watch your kids?
Or help you cook some food?
Do you need a night out with your significant other?
Do you need a night out with us?
What do you need?
What can we do?

I see the smile that you want to be real.
I know that you hoped I missed the emptiness I saw or the coldness behind the eyes.
But the truth is that I did see your fear and your disdain.
That was my call to help.
That was my cue to start a rescue mission.
That was my sign to start an intervention.
The intervention where we restore your faith in God,
Hope for the impossible, love for yourself, and
Trust in things and those who matter most.

I looked into those eyes the other day.
The hurt stayed on my mind.
Forgive me if we have overstepped our perceived boundaries but we are your real friends.
I would rather have you here and be able to make up from your scowl than not have you here at all.

Diva, we love you. Please let us help you.

STORM

You created a Storm
You named it me
Tropical Storm
Hurricane
Typhoon

Storm
Uncontrollable
Unforgettable
Unbelievable

You created a Storm
Named it me
Expect rain
       Some soft rains
Expect thunder
       Torrential rains
Sometimes lightening
Expect flooding
Seasonal, unexpected storms

You created a Storm
Named it me
Absolutely Amazing Storm
Truly Memorable Storm
News-making,
Record-breaking Storm
Powerful,
Overwhelming Storm

You created a Storm
Named it me
Me
Storm
Storms
Stormy
Storming

You created me
Storm is just an attitude

The Dynamic Of the Woman

The Dynamic of the Woman

dy·nam·ic *[dahy-nam-ik]*

–adjective Also, **dy·nam·i·cal.**
1. pertaining to or characterized by energy or effective action; vigorously active or forceful; energetic: *the dynamic president of the firm.*
2. *Physics.*
    a. of or pertaining to force or power.
    b. of or pertaining to force related to motion.

–noun
7. a basic or dynamic force, esp. one that motivates, affects development or stability, etc.

Oops, I Did It Again

I thought you were my safe place
But I made an assumption
You were to be my wise confidant
My emotional safe haven

How inconsiderate of me
Who knew I was yours
Your safe place
Your emotional refuge

The tension surfaced
When no one showed up for work
Everyone showed up to be showered
Each one prepared to be pampered
Each one expected to be spoiled

The tension festered
When I felt neglected
When I felt sacrificed
When I needed you yet silence
When I asked yet no answers received
When you insulted my intelligence with the charades
Nil sense
Non sense

He's driving me back to Him
       Through everyone I know
       Through every means possible

I apologize for holding you responsible for my needs
I am sorry I gifted you with the responsibility of my well-being
I regret to realize that my security was in
       Jeopardy with you at the helm
I consider myself a pearl and precious commodity
You can't throw precious items to swine
And expect awesome results

The fact is that you needed me exactly as I needed you
Your search resembles mine quite closely
—the one person that takes your breath away
—the single individual who helps your breaths matter
—the single individual who supports the value of your breaths
—the person who loves you in spite of yourself

Oops, I did it again.
I apologize for it happening to you

A Spectacular Failure

When I review the last several years
I define them as the most spectacular failure
I have yet to witness

Total loss—absolutely not!
Beautiful children
Educational accomplishments
Financial stress and strides
Stuff
Career achievements
Started several businesses
Not a total loss

When I review the last several years,
I discover I gave myself away
I gave up my stuff
I gave away more than I received

While this failed
I learned a lot
I survived
And so did you.

When you review our failed relationship
Consider the new possibilities
    —have it your way
The selfishness kept compounding like interest

Sure, living apart forever may be difficult
But living together seemed impossible
We will grow and learn
Succeed and thrive
Be better parents for them
Be better for others

This by far will be the most
Spectacular failure
We will ever experience

To end something which
Started so perfectly seems foolish
Not so much
Together, we had a failure to thrive
Apart, forces awesome results

Experienced the Spectacular Failure

YOUR EYES ... BUT

Your eyes didn't lie to me
    But your mouth did

Your eyes didn't decline me
    But your thoughts did

Your eyes didn't question me
    But your mind did

Your eyes said what you felt
    But your mouth didn't

Your eyes taught me to love you
    But your words didn't

Your eyes told me that you needed me
    But you would have me to believe otherwise

Your eyes suggested our future
    But you decided otherwise

Your eyes didn't deceive me
    But you did

SEPARATE AGENDAS

Different thoughts   different fears
Different backgrounds   different dreams
Different styles   different lives
Different tasks   different themes
                 Not the same page
                 Not the same pace
                 Not the same process
                 Not the same patience
                               A joined life
                               But separate agendas

Changing concepts
Mixed emotions
Unnecessary tifts
Separate and unequal
                 No way near
                 Not on the plane
                 Not even close
                 "Not so much"
                               Can you hear me now
                               Did you change networks
                               Can you hear me now
                               You used to hear me clearly
                               Now not at all

Joined lives need to share
                 The agenda

FROM ONE DROP TO A FLOOD

When that one drop
Transformed into
A drizzle,
What were you doing?

Could you be daydreaming
When you should be paying attention?
Could it be that the transformation
Was about your life?

When that drizzle became
A soft rain,
What were you thinking?
What did you think that meant?

Could you have been focused on the wrong thing?
What could've been more important than?
Could you have been focused at the wrong time?

When that soft rain started
To down pour,
How did you feel?

Did the overwhelming emotion overcome you?
Did the life you dreamed of come under fire?

When that downpour
Transitioned to drown a city
Did you reflect on what should have happened?
Could that flood have been prevented
At perhaps the drip
Or could it have been settled at the drizzle
Or maybe the soft rains should've arrested your attention
And certainly the downpour was obvious
Enough to center on changing
The direction of that tumultuous rain

So the rain has ceased
The flood waters have receded
The rain maker departed
Could being more conscious of the rain
Stop a drip from becoming a flood?

BECAUSE LEFTOVERS WON'T DO

Not after you wash the car
Nor after you watch football
    Or basketball
    Or hockey
    Or baseball
    Or golf
Not even after you bathe

Not after your mother
    Or mine
Not after my children
    Or yours
Not after your co-workers
    Or your class mates
    Or your enemies
Not after the church membership
    Or the perfect strangers

Can I be second
Only to Christ
Just would like my deserved position

Want second rather than last
Last gets leftovers
Leftover time
Leftover conversation
Leftover energy
    Sometimes there isn't anything left for me
Leftovers won't do

THE DEFINITION OF A LITTLE WHILE

From one minute to forty-five
It is clear that we differ on our definition of
A little while

A short time period versus long
But what defines long versus short
Define a little while

When you said a little while
I thought you meant a few minutes
Yet hours resulted

When you suggested a little while
I waited and waited
As you baited me along
For days at a time

Define a little while
      A few minutes or several hours
      A couple of days or a week
      This year or in five
      This decade or next
Surely you can understand why I need
You to define a little while

My heart is at stake
Not yours

You said that you loved me
You promised me your heart
In a little while
I have yet to receive said love
Or specified heart

I just need to know if I should wait
A little while
Using my definition
Or yours

Please define a little while

A Fragile Marriage

On a single thread
The strongest, single thread
Maybe silk
Adding threads not easy
Not sure how single arrived
When others were present

The threads of communication missing first
Long silences
No eye contact
Sharp comebacks
My way, not yours
Lies
Broken promises
Begging

The thread of trust missing next
Alone
Lonely
Loner
Disbelief
More lies

The thread of companionship exchanged for others
Family
Friends
Work
School
How long would she be last, really?

The other threads loosed and broken
Randomly and systematically
The human body shuts down in the same manner
One organ signals the others to shut down
Once that process starts, reversal nearly impossible

This fragile marriage
Survived many small storms
Hurricane toppled the relationship
Several other storms hit before repair could begin
Recently declared disaster area
Aid declined

A fragile, fragile marriage
One thread away from dissolve
Too many threads to healing
Once on the same road
Now on such different paths
That those paths never intersect again.

When your lifetime plans changes course
This fragile marriage ends.

A once strong marriage
Suffered irreversible damage
Turned fragile
Suffered involuntary damage
Made weak
Unrecoverable

                A Fragile Marriage indeed

COVENANT UNDER SCRUTINY

I stopped talking
We stopped talking
We stopped loving
I stopped trusting you
I stopped believing that we would make it
You added to my hurt
I'd rather you soothe my hurt than add to it
You stole my excitement and fragile stability
You took my fantasy
I realized that I didn't like being at home
I didn't rush to make a decision because
        I didn't want to make a mistake
        I didn't want to change my mind
I lost my comfort zone
My guard, "Fort Knox" returned
I lost my desire to be with you
I lost my desire to be committed
Broken promises

We Exhausted the Possibilities

Where did the time go?
    The time we once spent together
    The time we spent on us and only us

Where did the tenderness go?
    The tender words we once shared
    The tender glances we once exchanged

Where did the love go?
    The love that inspired others
    The love that defined poetry

Where did the laughter go?
    The authentic laughter which speaks volumes
    The authentic laughter which cancelled misunderstandings

Where did the sacrifice go?
    The sacrifices which communicated care
    The sacrifices which communicated concern

Where did the romance go?
    The romance that stimulated the conversation which led to lovemaking
    The romance which sent flowers and cooked dinner

When did the conversation stop?
    The conversations that once were the catalyst for relations
    The conversations that once were the source of promises

When did the silence start?
    Silence is okay now, not before
    Silence stimulates distance

When did the lovemaking stop?
    The gentleness stopped
    The touching ceased

When did the resentment start?
    The resentment brought the bitterness
    The resentment introduced the hurt

When did the love stop?
    The missing love stopped my heart
    The missing love created the pain

When did we exhaust the possibilities?
    The possibilities designed to lead us together
    The possibilities which existed for the rest of our lives.

We exhausted the possibilities of a lifetime.

WITH A HARDENED HEART

I try to love you
In spite of a hardened heart
Hurt, harm and neglect
Breakthrough looks bleak

I try to love you
With all of my broken heart
Pieces too far apart
Breakthrough looks bleak

I try to love you
Stone hard heart
Glossy concrete found in model home
Breakthrough looks bleak

I try to love you
Chisel away the pieces
Bring together the brokenness
Is breakthrough possible?
Yes or no

I try to love you
I hear your voice
I feel your heart
I know you want to be different
But no guarantees
Outlook is bleak

With a hardened heart
So hard to endure
Heart so broken
Need tape and glue and glitter and thread
Never seamless again

With a hardened heart
Love hard to generate
Hard to conjure
Hard to contemplate
Hard to feel
Hard to love

ENDINGS

Maybe it ended because she stopped reading her poetry at bedtime to him
Maybe it was because he stopped listening

Or it could be ending because she never let herself become self absorbed

Or it could be over because they lost sight of the vision

Well, it could've ended because he was waiting for her to be quiet
Also, the end could've been a result of her sudden, intense silence

At any rate, her intense silence and his complacent waiting resulted in the end

While silence had been previously desired, he begs desperately for it to end—she misunderstands and ends the relationship rather than the silence

In court we would need documentation but how do you document the loss
Of the second element of the relationship
      When did he really do it and when did she follow suit?

All in all, the summation is these two have forgotten where they began so they strayed
They strayed so far and when they finally realized it, they couldn't find their way back.

Still it has yet to be determined whether or not they exhausted all the possibilities,
Yet the end is reached.

Is This A Test of Will

Is this a question of if I love him
After all is said and done
Then he'll concede
His soul
His spirit
His body
He'll even concede his love

Is this a test of wills
My will
My perseverance
My ability to outlast
His mask
His strategy
His tests of my intentions

He says he loves
Yet I am at his arm's length and mine

Is this a competition to see
Who will be standing
When all is said and done

Is this designed to test my will
My spirit
My love
My decision making
My heart

Is he building trust
Or testing for loyalty
Could this be his mask
Being tested
Test my will other ways
I love you
And always will.

NO PROMISES REQUIRED

Don't make me any promises
        Especially ones you cannot keep

Keep your false statements
        For your own self-gratification

The last promises you made
        Are yet driving grief

When you "promise"
        You entered a covenant
        Your covenant credit has been revoked

Your promises resemble proposals
        Proposals which fail at presentation

No promises required
Keeps you honest
Lowers the standard which introduced lies in the first place

No promises, please
No time to discern the ridiculous
No desire to unravel the mystery
No need to elevate the otherwise complicated

Please, No Promises

ON YOUR TERMS

ONLY on your terms
ALWAYS on your terms
No room left for me
Your way or the highway
Regardless of the viability
Or credibility
Or the dependability
Regardless of the proof

Only on your terms
Without regard for another
No listening
No talking
These unattractive, non-negotiable terms
So unbearable
So unreasonable
Wildly distressing

Only on your terms
Ideas threatened
Or position
Yet no forward movement
Without your seal
Without your invitation
Without your initiation
Without variation
Without theme

These unattractive, non-negotiable terms
So labor-intensive
So selfish
So consumed
So closed
Completely singular
No growth
No leadership
No partnership
No worthy opposition
Not even the devil's advocate is considered

On your terms
Leaves no room for me
      Or any other

Always on your terms

HIS/HERS

Now since the issues have somewhat pre-sorted themselves,
Let's examine the issues seemingly unconquerable
>> It was his lack of commitment
>> It was her lack of trust
>> It was his lack of attentiveness
>> It was her lack of communication
>> It was his lack of intensity
>> It was her aggressive nature
>> It was his passive silence
>> It was her silence
>> It was his talkative nature
>> It was her inability to forgive
>> It was their lack of passion
>>>> Passion essential to the survival of any love.

EXPECT SOME CONSEQUENCES

Consequences
Little
Great
Minimal
Monumental
Expect them

Neglect
Negligence
Malice
Ill-intent
Irreparable damage
Unforgiveness
Forgetfulness
Negativity
Naïveté

Consequences
Catastrophic
Climatic
Consecutive
Consequential
Expect them

Unprepared
Underprepared
Selfish
Selfishly
Selfishness
Foolish
Near-sighted
Sidetracked
Incomprehensible
Incoherent
Irresponsible

Consequences
Imminent
Irreversible
Intentional
Irrevocable
Expect them
. . . All of them

THE STARTING FIVE

A team designed to maintain a diva
A team composed to support the woman
A team planned to cater to High Maintenance

Acquaintance
>> Not close but flirts
>> Enhances the self-esteem
>> Co-signs on the image
>> Disapproves of the "off-days"

Confidant
>> Best friend
>> Knows the low days before they land
>> Seeks the meaning behind the façade
>> Reads the mind and is accurate
>> Chick-flick movie mate
>> Power partner
>> Business resource

Spiritual partner
>> Prayer partner
>> Study partner
>> Accountability partner
>> Co-laborer in discipleship

Lover
>> Reads the poetry
>> Rubs the feet
>> Caresses the hair
>> Stares during the soft snores
>> Driver during the storms
>> Comfort for the ridiculous

And then there's you
>> . . . the Husband
Reaping the benefit of the hardwork
The cooking and the cleaning
You don't mind because
You are too tired
>> To talk and pray
>> To spoil and treat
>> To travel and listen
>> To remember and respond
>> To support and study

You are glad because
You don't have the energy
To maintenance the diva.

So who's on your team?
And whose team are you on?

WALKED AWAY

He spit statements designed
To wilt her self-esteem

Statements designed to start a storm
That he didn't realize would rain on him

He rushed to judge rather than listen
Only to find himself speaking into a mirror

He snapped to argue the mute point
And found that she was no longer listening

He clings to the past
Only to realize that she is now absent from the present

He chastised her for needing him
Which he later regrets because she is gone

He thinks he is hurting her with his words
While she moves out of range of the sound of this voice

He holds her this distance
And then she walked away.

HIDE AND SEEK

Qualities hidden in your mate
Seek them in the other

What a game we play with another's life
When we seek to fulfill our desires
When we are unhappy and
Hide in the arms of another

Hidden are the eyes
        Full of hurt and pain
Seeking comfort
        Seek comfort
        See comfort

Do you seek the hurts of your mate
Do you hide your hurts from your mate

Do you seek to hurt your mate
Do you hide from your mate to avoid hurt

The game needs closure
Hide and seek

Seek your mate
Seek the details of that mate
Seek to heal the hurts of your mate

Hide the hurt
Seek to heal
Seek to forgive
Seek to build that relationship

Don't hide
Seek

LOVE LETTER

Thank you for thinking of me
        And keeping me at a distance
        So that I don't get hurt

I know I keep asking for the same things
        —that's what I need
        Or so I thought.
The wonderful thing about the truth
        Is that it doesn't require a memory.

Thank you for sparing me
        The investment
        The energy
            Of loving you
            Without love in return

Although this distance seems effective
        It was initiated too late.

I am already in love.
Too late to reverse the feelings, emotions, investments.

Too late to recall the letter . . .
        This is not email.

Distance is better?

I wrote you a love letter
        With my time
        When I compliment you
        Because I complement you
        Through my energy
        Through my trust
        From my efforts
        When I share
        Because I feed you

I write you a love letter
Often

Too late to recall the letter
This is my heart
        . . . not email.

SAN ANTONIO, TEXAS

Baby, please don't leave me—
Please don't go
I fear that I'll lose you,
That our love will be lost forever.
I'm grasping for time,
Time to show you how deep my feelings are for you.
Am I being selfish?
Can you understand that you are leaving,
Because you must, not because you want to
But I wish it could be some other way.
I fear that you'll never return—
That we will never be together again.

I need you
Okay, I said it
Baby, please don't leave me
I beg you not to go.

CONDITIONAL LOVE

Love
Love at will
Love with contingencies
Love with just cause
Love under stipulations
Love on loan
Love with strings

Love conditionally
Love on the condition of
Love based on other criteria, standards and stuff

Love in need of maintenance
Love in need of tender love and care

Real love only exists
Without conditions
Or strings
Or theories
And without restrictions
      Or what if
      Or if . . . then
      Or if and only if . . . then
Conditional ends quickly
With condition

I cannot breathe under
Conditional love
I cannot survive with
Conditional love

Thanks for the conditional love
But no thanks
Conditional love is not enough
Conditional love does not satisfy
Conditional love leaves me empty

Conditional love is not enough

The Dreams Of the Woman

The Dreams of the Woman

Dream [dreem]

—noun
1. a succession of images, thoughts, or emotions passing through the mind during sleep.
2. the sleeping state in which this occurs.
3. an object seen in a dream.
4. an involuntary vision occurring to a person when awake.
5. a vision voluntarily indulged in while awake; daydream; reverie.
6. an aspiration; goal; aim: *A trip to Europe is his dream.*
7. a wild or vain fancy.
8. something of an unreal beauty, charm, or excellence.

—verb (used without object)
9. to have a dream.
10. to indulge in daydreams or reveries: *He dreamed about vacation plans when he should have been working.*
11. to think or conceive of something in a very remote way (usually fol. by *of*): *I wouldn't dream of asking them.*

—verb (used with object)
12. to see or imagine in sleep or in a vision.
13. to imagine as if in a dream; fancy, suppose.
14. to pass or spend (time) in dreaming (often fol. by *away*): *to dream away the afternoon.*

THE FIRST LADY

First in your life
First as your wife

The one you think of first
Consider first

The one you sacrifice for first
She is first

The first lady
Defined
Refined
Intelligent
Humorous
Beautiful

Your top priority
After your Lord and Master
Not after your peoples
Not beyond your children
First
Your First Lady

The First Lady
Of your life
Your bride
Your lover
Your wife

Treat her special
    Because she deserves
Respect her
    Because she is
Protect her
    Because she needs your covering
Love your first lady
    As the gift she is

The FIRST Lady
The First LADY
YOUR first Lady

Second to God
She is first.

BEAUTIFUL CHEMISTRY

Ever seen two people
Who were moving
In such a motion
That you realized
They were special
From across the room

Ever witnessed
Artful conversation
Reaching resolve
Melting hearts
Mending fences
Meeting needs

Ever wondered
How two sensitive people
Meet
Relate
Dismiss the distractions
Commit

Ever envied
The relationship
Where you heard authentic laughter
Felt genuine love
Experienced complete forgiveness
Enhanced spiritual maturity

Ever occurred that
Powerful relationships
Are born to
Beautiful chemistry
Beautiful chemistry
Made with you.

LOVE ETHIC

When I consider the love in my life
I consider your love ethic
Like work ethic
I hung that sign
With the intention to attract
A bold, handsome man
Attentive and energetic
Considerate and supportive
Responsive and kind
Meek and gentle
Strong and resourceful
Massaging my soul with his voice
Meeting my needs
Managing my fears
Mating on a new plateau
Minding my mind
Mending my hurts
I hang that sign with care
My strong, powerful love
A great steward required
A strong love ethic required
Not just anyone can manage this love
Not just anyone can minister to my spirit
Not just any being can survive my demands
No simple being will facilitate my expectations
It is an exhibit of love ethic
A profound love ethic
A never tiring
Ready to sweat
Going the extra distance
Which is often further than the next mile
Healthy, hearty love ethic
That never quits
A love ethic that weathers storms.
A love ethic love me completely,
      Fully
      Profoundly
      Unselfishly
And, uncontrollably,
A love ethic required.

GREAT MUSIC

Did that strike a chord
Did that chord strike a nerve
Did that melody penetrate your heart
Did that ballad induce a spell
When that note reached my soul
        A question was answered
When that tune reached my heart
        A yearning was massaged
When that chorus reached the recesses of my mind
        A love was remembered

I like the music which stirs the deepest emotion
That's the music that reignites love
Which was forgotten and dismissed

I like the music that causes the soul to pause and consider the purpose of a song

I like the music which influences the calm spirit within

I like the music which stirs the deepest emotion,
Reminds me to love,
Causes me to stand still,
Renders me speechless,
        —have you ever seen me speechless?
That's enough for you to love that music, too.

THE TRUTH IS

All of my poems are starting to
Sound the same
About how I'm going to love you
Care for you

But my momma always said
You don't have to remember the truth
When it's true, whether it splashes out
Or gushes out
Or oozes out
It covers you
Entirely

The memorable truth is
Better than the
Conjured fantasy

The truth and the heart are
Matched
The truth rests in the root of the heart
A memorable truth
Everlasting truth.

REMINDED

Raspy voice intimacy suggestive
Falling fall leaves
Long walks
Longer talks   museum
Later nights   museums
Indifferent   mused
Differences   amused
                        Zoo

Reminded of you

Is that you
Or only an image of you
I've created

IT'S YOU I CRAVE

My heart misbehaves
At the sound of your voice
My heart misbehaves
In response to your hug
My heart misbehaves
Because it's you I crave
    Yes the cliché
        I crave your presence

My body misbehaves
Under your touch
My body challenges me
When you are not nearby
Requesting your immediate attention
My body misbehaves
Underneath yours
Exchanging trade secrets
My body misbehaves
Because it's you crave
    Yes the cliché
        I crave your presence

My mind races
When we talk
My mind craves your intellect
My mind craves your thoughts, and feedback
    Wit and wisdom
        Comedic and therapeutic
My mind responds (in kind) with
        Imagery and poetry
        Dreams and aspirations
        Honesty and character

It's you I crave
Skips a beat for you
My heart flutters upon contact with yours

It's you I crave
Heart
Mind
Body

Craving you.

UNFORGIVING RULES

The rules say don't tell the whole truth
Tell something other than the truth

The rules say don't tell him you love him
But absolutely do

They say don't show him your "A" game
But I want to

The rules dictate not too close
But I want so close

I want to wake up next to him
After a wonderful night of lovemaking
And after our worst fight

I want him to soak my hair
All of it
The rules say not too close
        Not too soon
        Not too much

Did the rule writer EVER fall in love?
Is the rule writer in love now?
Does the rule writer know what love is?
I call for a rewrite of the rules
Or I'm gonna write my own!

POURING RAINS

Soft rain pours
Really pours
Sleep overcomes me
Quiet rain
Enticing rain
Seductive rain
Softness overwhelms me
Thoughts of you surface
Your voice speaks to me
Smile through the rain
The soft rain lulls me
The soft rains soothes me
The soft rain arouses me
The soft rain awakens me
I still need you
I still seek you
I still want you
Pouring rains
Stimulate thoughts of you

A Penny for Your Thoughts

Would a penny do
For you to share your thoughts with me
Oh please share
Your precious thoughts
A penny may not do
For me to earn your trust
But oh share the special memories
Your mind houses
A penny is all I have

I am the richest possession I possess
Am "I" enough to earn your thoughts
Am "I" enough to hear your memories
Am "I" enough to share your feelings
Am "I" enough to learn your needs
Am "I" enough to manage your trust
Am "I" enough to safe keep your secrets
Am "I" enough to dry your tears
Am "I" enough to receive your love
Oh please share
Your precious thoughts
A penny I don't have

I have only me
The me who wants to know you
The me who wants to know your dreams
The me who wants to empathize with you
The me who wants to know what makes you tick and
What ticks you off
I have only me
I want your thoughts
A penny won't do
Am "I" enough

THE TIME TO LOVE

The most important thing we have ever shared
        Is time
The kiss
The hug
        Both great but not the same

So special the time we have shared
The travel
The play
        Both great but not more than

The time we share provides power
The meals
The water
        Both great yet missing that power

The time we share defines our love
The talks
The walks
        Both wonderful yet missing the same weight

The most important thing we have ever shared
        Is time
We took the time to love
We share our lives in prayer
We spread our joy in service
We lend our hearts with joy
We seek the others' smile

The time it takes to love is time well spent
The time to love is the most important thing
        We have ever done

The time to love

Could you think of a better way to spend your time?

YOUR TRANSPARENCY

Your nakedness
    Intrigues me
Your honesty
    Inspires me
Your candor
    Influences me
Your intellect
    Invites me
Your voice
    Insulates me
Your transparency
    Is evident
    So very clear
You share
    Your inner most
You share
    Your deepest
You share
    Your love
    Through your transparency
Your transparency
    Draws me closer to you
When I know the you
    That I see
    Is real
When I know the you
    That I hear
    Is true
When I know the you
    That I touch
    Is authentic
I fall in love over and over
    Again
I love you

THE TENSION

The beautiful tension that exists
Between two
        A wondering two
        A magnetic two
        An elusive two
        A dynamic two

The mysterious tension
That draws two together
        A wandering two
        A powerful two
        A passionate two
        A creative two

The unbearable tension
        When our eyes meet
        And our expressions change
        When that hug creates the electricity
        And drives the pressure

The creative tension
        His voice
        Her writings
        His service
        Her education
        His playtime
        Her vacations

The anticipated tension
        Which exists
        Between lovers
        Between friends
        Between soul mates
        Between life partners
        Between two

The silent tension
Solved
Yet intensified
When they meet
When they join
When they speak
When they hug
When they dance
When they love
When they play
When they bathe
When they sleep
When they share

DANGEROUS

"loving you and having you is two different things." r.w.

Oh I absolutely love you
Truly
Passionately
Unconditionally
Without one doubt

Completely in love with you
Extremely
Decisively
Profoundly
Beyond the shadow of that doubt

Comprehensively loving you is my desire
My dream
My hope
My prayer
Powerful loving that would last a lifetime

Such a promise of a powerfully
Passionate and complete love

Having you—well not exactly possible

You wear this sign—
Caution
Proceed with care
DANGEROUS

You have these limitations—
      Tots
      Platinum
      Address

I have these fears—
      Loving you but not having you
      Wanting you but rejected
      Needing you but denied

So when I said loving you and having you was two different things,
I meant I love you but I can't seem to have you. Notify me as soon as that changes. I want us. I need you. I love you, and have for quite awhile now. Just want to love you all the time.

I want to have You—All of you!

BECAUSE OF...
YOU

I listen to different music
And more of it
I eat different foods
And enjoy them
I changed my hair
And I like it
I know love exists
And I want more of it
I feel like loving again
And it excites me
I stopped the negative self-talk
And I feel great about me
I quit the bitterness
And it feels great
I smile
And I smile big
I laugh
And I laugh loudly
I live authentically
And I live well
I spend more time praying
And I have peace
I like spending time alone
And I like me—I just realized
I know that I am worth it
And worth all of it
I appreciate quiet dinners
And the silence doesn't hurt
I learned that life is really short
And I need to live it fully
I keep my promises
And I always will
I need love
And I crave you

Because of you
Life is different and refreshing
Life is wonderful and exciting

Because of you
Love is the best thing that ever happened to me
Love is worth the chance
Love is worth the lifetime that
Love takes to join two hearts

Because of You.

BETWEEN THE DROPS

One drop
Two
Three
More
Drizzle
Drop
Downpour

Can I move around between the raindrops?
I would name the drops if I could
Each one realizes its role in my life
Each one recognizes its role to life

Drops
Destined to fall

When the drops drench me
I relax
I unwind
Close my eyes
Breathe in deep

When the drops cover me
Vulnerability starts
Infatuation seeps in
Care spills over
Distance evaporates

When the drops cleanse me
      Speechlessness
                ness
                ness
Desire splashes out
Discipline escapes

When the drops cleave to me
Love drowns me
My spirit lifts
Clarity found
Creativity awakened

Between the drops that drench me
      I smile
      I laugh
      I cry
      I live
      I love

INTIMATE DISTANCE

Those elusive eyes entice me
From a distance once
Closer and closer now
The eyes lure me closer
The smile speaks to me
Inviting me in the inner circle
The inner circle houses love
The inner circle frames the heart

The distance between your heart and mine
Shaped by intimacy
The distance we create
Through barriers and lies
Through secrets and misunderstandings
Through actions and attitudes

Intimacy grows with time
Intimate touch
Intimate listening
Intimate destinations
The intimate distance
Shortened by trust and pillow talk

The difference between your heart and mine
       Shaped by intimacy

Pull me closer to you
Move me closer to your heart
Hold me close

Intimate space critical
Intimate time valuable
Intimacy crucial

In to me see equals intimacy
Close the distance
The intimate distance should be close
Should be closed

I just love you
I just need you
Just keep looking through me intimately
Intimate glances

THE LOOK SAID IT ALL

There are looks between lovers
Differing from friends
From intimate glances
To the complete smile

When a simple smile could do
Lovers offer precious glances
Glances which invite them together
Glances which promises rendezvous
Glances which communicates understanding
Glances which speaks care

When she closed her eyes after her eyes met his
Her blush complexion confirmed her desire
His flush countenance confirmed his tension

She opened her eyes
They bat uncontrollably
Sharing her deep desire
Exposing her longing

The look said it all
How she feels
What she wants
What she needs

There are looks between lovers
Differing between friends
His look closed the distance from across the room
Every smile brings them closer

The look said it all
Speaks volumes
Speaks love
Speaks intensity

There are looks between lovers

HAND OVER THE TROPHY

The standard to measure others
The mold by which others are made
Beauty walking
Brilliance talking
Prior labels replaced by TROPHY

Trophy?

Trophy friend?
Trophy wife?
Trophy what?

Accomplished
Achiever
Beautiful
Bold
Classic
Classy
Cute
Daring
Decisive
Demanding
Direct

Definition of trophy
A half match
The look
The physique
The laugh
Sure they fit
The substance
The ambition
The drive
The wisdom
Obvious mismatch

Trophy on display
Dusted every so often
Sometimes forgotten
Trophies replaced often

The wisdom
The look
The laugh
The zeal
The refreshing

The trophy admired   but at a distance
The trophy respected   but from afar

The Measure of a Woman

Envy the trophy   up close and personal

Trophy looks?
Trophy attitude?
Trophy what?

Distinct
Driven
Fly
Honest
Integrity
Intensity
Jazzy
Leader
Modern
Optimistic
Over-achiever

Trophy search
    Endless and unfulfilled
Trophy care
    Neglect and burdened

Why trophy?
Trophy what?

Perfectionist
Polished
Radiant
Radical
Refreshing
Relevant
Sassy
Sexy
Snazzy
Substantive
Traditional

Hand over the trophy
Fragile—handle with care

LOVERS DON'T QUARREL

No fighting
No quarreling
No bartering
Lovers just don't do
Just sweet talk
Kiss
Kissing
Kisses
Hugs
Moans
Groans
No dishes
No laundry
No mopping
No bills
Just play time
With bathing
More play time
Play
Play
Play
No children
No in-laws
No rules
No holidays
No boundaries
No groceries
Just sighs
And laughs
And giggles
Some tickling
And squealing
No issues
No tissues
No whining
No mood swings
No attitudes
No anger
No criticism
Just your best
Wonder
Amazement
Excitement
Just the best
Only love
No quarreling

IN THE PRESENCE OF THE PRESENT

In front of me you stand
Genuine laughter and all
Meek and wild
Yielding and coy
In my ear you whisper
My name passionately
With such deep intensity
Gifting me with love
Spoiling me
Attending to my moans
Responding to my needs
In front of me you stand
Questioning glance
Weary eyes
Is this where my love lies
The truest of love
The deepest of passion
The intensity of trust
In front of me you stand
Collecting my thoughts
Observing my desires
Inviting my attention to your best work
Kissing my senses peaked
My gift to you—me
In my presence—we
In the Presence of the Present

You Started It

That's how it all starts
Love, I mean
A smile
A glance
Eye-contact—pure, pensive, piercing
And skirts, plenty of skirts
The power of femininity
Jump starts love like you wouldn't believe
Hair, beautiful
And if you can get the authentic laughter
Love is in the air and on its way around the corner
Believe me I know how it all starts
But conversation is key
Ask
Listen
Compliment
Remember
The details
Treat conversation like your best investment
Then ask
Listen
Compliment
Remember
Exclusively the details
Until she says yes
Until she loves you completely and
Unconditionally
Until she misses you
Until she seeks you
Until she craves your touch
Until she needs you
Then never stop
See that's how love starts
Begin love
Beginning love never ends
Real love
Genuine love
Passionate love
      . . . never dies
Remember how love starts and
    Do it over and over again.

INSTANT LOVE

A deep rich instant love
Love at first sight
It happens
Truer still than ordinary love

Not the add sugar and stir love
But the love that comes from prayer

I instantly love you
My eyes met yours
A love so true and real
Evolved
Before my unbelieving eyes

Your warm embrace
Your infinite wisdom
Your powerful pride
All speak volumes

A relinquishing love
Instant chemistry
A moment's notice

An instant and rich love
Unfailing
Profoundly powerful
Proof of answered prayer
I love you.

THE STATE OF THE RELATIONSHIP ADDRESS

Commitment to each other
Commitment to God
Finances
Communication
Trust (past and present)
Church
Respect
Appreciation
Double-standard
Studying together
Do you know your mate
My garbage
My prayers
The me you may not like—are you going to love me anyway
The history and transformation of this relationship
Yet to be transformed and transitioned
Forgiveness
Help mate
A working relationship with respect and privacy
Without interference, advice, consultation

THE TESTER BOTTLE

The fragrance in each bottle different
The herbs and flowers and oils
—All different
Different increments
Mixed differently to create different smells
No fragrance smells the same
So we try several until
We find a match
We smell the bottle first
Then we spray a little on
Then we wave the spot
    To temper the fragrance
When we smell it
    We close our eyes to enjoy the
        Whole experience
    We inhale deeply to appreciate how it makes us feel
If we fall in love with the fragrance
    We purchase it and take it home
    We may wear it extensively
    Or we may work it into the rotation
We may repeat this process several times
Until that one fragrance that you can't stop thinking about
The one fragrance that you absolutely love and adore
The one fragrance which makes you feel so good
    That you forsake it for all others
When you don't wear it you seem lost
    For That fragrance is your signature fragrance
    Reinforces your confidence
    Enhances your self-esteem
    Considers your feelings
When the fragrance loves you back
    Wholly, completely, forever
You stop testing fragrances
You stop looking at tester bottles

TRUER STILL

If I could be true to you
        About my feelings
And truer still about my words
Would I draw you closer
Or move you from my person completely

Do you really want to know how I feel
That sometimes I hate you
Often I love you
I was angry yesterday
I need you to rub my feet

Do you need to know that I dreamed of our intimacy
I woke up looking for you
When spending the rest of my life with you seems difficult
I stay anyway
I love our spiritual life
I want more baths or showers or just water

I want to cook more
I want to play more
And talk more
I want your promises to be true
Are you closer still
Or will I see you never?

LOOKING AROUND FOR LOVE

Love
Who can find
Such riches elude me
So much mystery to deliver love to me
Why search
Why seek
Not sure to find
Not sure to meet
Define love anyway
Too detailed
Too sensitive
Too demanding
Too time consuming
Too much investment
Need love
        Or just want
Want love
        Or just lonely
Seek love
        Or just bored
Find love
        Or just tired
Of looking around at the illusion of the best
        Emotional roller coaster you may never ride
Such riches continue to elude me

TIMING IS EVERYTHING

The difference between me
Spending my afternoon with a
Single man and that married one
Was that dry conversation

Someone is going to come along
Designed to love me
So no thanks, I'll just wait

You sent me this storm
Now fix me
You sent this storm
Named it me
Now fix me

Where is my angel?
The exact one who says the
Exact thing at that the most
Awesome moment

Timing is indeed everything
I'll just wait

GOOD EYES

Used them to access your soul
Examining the depth and breadth of your soul
Examining for spirit or sultan
Cross referencing for passion and perseverance

Used them to match my desires
And your capabilities
Checked the boxes
Confirmed the similarities

Used them to seek your heart
Measure its love capacity
Searched for signs of compassion
Seeking a shared space for a union of those hearts

Used them to explore your mind
Questioning the intellect, wit, wisdom
Hoping for ultimate truth, game-free
Clarifying the clarity of thought process: can you think?

Used them to experience the charming personality
Explored it for authenticity
Expected system failure
However all systems were a go for launch

The good eyes cleared you
The first question is for what—what will happen
Is it good for the eyes
Secondly, when will it happen
Is the "what" timely for the eyes
Then, how
    Will the good eyes receive what they saw?
        Regularly, consistently, genuinely?
Then, why
    Because the eyes have spotted what they want exactly
    Beyond a shadow of a doubt
    Beyond the reasonable doubt that does exist.
Lastly, where
    Will the good eyes find authentic love with you
    The pure, true, real, refreshing, sacrificial,
        Unconditional love with you

Need answers
Need the truth
Good eyes cannot afford any errors.

ACROSS THE SPECTRUM

She doesn't compartmentalize well, if at all

You could move across all of the
        Relational categories by lunch
        And you would never know

She may move you there to the
        Premium: "Husband"
        All in her mind

She moves you across this relationship spectrum
        And moves you back across that same spectrum
        During a bath or a stroll or pedicure

She wants you
        She dreams of the potential of you
            She needs you
                She cares for you
                      She cares about you

She seeks your attention
She risks her life for you
She doesn't want to disappoint you

She wants access to your heart
She wants access to your soul
She needs your reassurance
She needs your leadership

She invites you across that spectrum
She invites you to explore that spectrum
She invites you to BE that spectrum

MY SAFE PLACE

I want the circle your arms form
To be my safe place
Absolutely not fair
Absolutely not your job
Security by request
Security by demand

The circle . . .
    Warm
    Tender
    Special
    Curious

The circle . . .
    Comfortable
    Wise
    Sensitive
    Charming

I want the circle your arms to form
A hedge of protection around me
Offering a profound peace
Labeled my safe place
My refuge from the ridiculous
My strength in weakness
My shelter from the storm

My Safe Place . . . The Circle Your Arms Form

My escape from the mundane
    The outlandish
    The mediocre
    The pain

Neither refugee
None stranger
But haven for your only love
    Only lover
    Best friend
    Confidant
    Special

Where I make you secure too.

IN

What does it cost you to let her in?
Much, little or nothing?
Begging for access.

Access: denied!

But why?
You invited her to the window
But that was far enough

What happened?
Were the questions too probing
Were the answers too tough

When she explored your heart
Did she frighten you
Did she cause you to pause
Did you witness parts of you that
        You hadn't intended to disclose

She just wants in
That's too much?

In.
In your life.
In your space.
In your heart.
In your eyes.
In your spirit.
In your mind.
In your soul.

She wants in—
Please

What is it going to cost you?
Oh love—it might cost you
Time or love or other precious commodities
You cherish more than her

Try it out
Let her in
You might like her in
Then you could relax
It requires more energy to keep her out
It costs you more to keep her out
Than to let her in

Just let her in

THE MEASURE OF A WOMAN

The Measure of a Woman
    What is the width of her spirit
    What is the depth of her mind
    What is the weight of her heart
    What is the volume of her body
    What is the capacity of her mind
    What is the speed of her thoughts
    What is the circumference of her hugs
    What is the breadth of her love
    How many inches does she let you within the boundaries of her heart
    How many feet until she reaches forgiveness
    What is the slope of her attitude
    What is the velocity of her meekness

The Measure of a Woman
    She thinks critically
    She plans carefully
    She speaks dynamically
    She loves passionately
    She lives authentically
    She moves fearlessly
    She leads humbly
    She fears God

Experience the Measure of a Woman
    Her love
    Her fears
    Her tears
    Her victories
    Her power
    Her influence
    Her motivation

Invest in the Measure of a Woman
    Create for her a loving environment
    Create for her a safe place

Go the distance for the Measure of a Woman
The Measure of a Woman
    Defines love
    Defies opposition
    Declares independence
    Decorates hearts
    Demands chemistry

The Measure of a Woman

ACKNOWLEDGEMENTS

God, thank You for Your plans for me. Thank You for ***The Measure of a Woman*** and choosing me to complete Your project. I just want to please You. Thank You for continuing to anoint me and to invest in me and my gifts, which keep surprising me. Thank You for loving and forgiving me.

Hillary and Nehemiah, thank you for enduring my late nights, your ideas, the sounding board, the love and the support. Thank you for loving me, especially when I do nothing without a pen and a clipboard. Family, thank you for supporting me and my endeavors.

To my editor, Ronald Williams. Thanks for the feedback and the discussions. The bantering has grown me and my writing. Thanks for enforcing the standard. Thank you for raising the bar of standards.

To my graphic artist, Ron Nicholson and Picture Perfect Designs. Thanks for the art and imagination, for making my words look fabulous.

To my prayer partners and to my accountability partners, thank you for the long talks and the powerful prayers and the encouragement.

To the women who this will reach and empower and touch and affect, may these words empower you and help you reach some resolve. May you be inspired to achieve your goals and dreams. May you enhance your relationship with God so that your other relationships will also improve. May you enhance your self-esteem through prayer and study. May you have courage and peace. Share love the best you can until you can share love without reservation.

About the Author

Minister Onedia N. Gage has been writing since age 13. She encourages the creativity in others and is a consultant for those who write. She desires to turn what has previously been a hobby into full-time career.

Her life philosophy is three – fold: A) "What have you done today to invest in your future?" B) Reading is essential to your positive contribution to our community; and, C) "If not me, who? If not now, when?" She feels her time is best spent when youth benefit from her experiences.

She created Purple Ink, Incorporated, to serve as publishing and promotional company for her writing and public speaking. Purple Ink also does ghostwriting, consulting, and publishing for the general public. Recently, Purple Ink established a foundation to provide funding for youth educational organizations and battered women's shelters.

Minister Gage answered her calling as a minister in October, 2003, and was licensed June, 2009, at Wheeler Avenue Baptist Church. She is an active member of The Church Without Walls where is on the clergy team, the women's ministry, children's ministry and Vacation Bible School, and facilitates the Christian education.

Because of her commitment to youth and community, she facilitates youth enrichment workshops. She believes that while exposure to certain things is common in other cultures, in the African American community, it is a special occasion. She uses these opportunities to encourage our youth to succeed. Other workshops she teaches "Nobel Woman Stand," "New Year, New You," "Choosing God's Best," and "If Not Me, Who? If Not Now, When?" In addition, she facilitates Vacation Bible Schools, retreats and lock-ins, specific to communication and group dynamics for young people and women.

Because of her volunteerism with the Houston Area Urban League's NULITES, she was elected one of the youngest board members of the Houston Area Urban League. She is also a member of Zeta Phi Beta Sorority, Inc., Top Ladies of Distinction, National Council of Negro Women, Toastmasters, International, and "Sistah to Sistah," a literary review group.

Onedia N. Gage is a native Houstonian. She is a graduate of Kaplan University with a Masters in Business Administration, and the University of Houston, central campus, with a Bachelor's of Science degree in Economics and a minor in African American Studies. She is a graduate of Bellaire Senior High School. She is currently pursuing her Master's in Education in Education Administration and Ph. D. in Business Leadership.

She has a daughter, Hillary Nicole, and a son, Nehemiah Christian.

ISBN: 978-0-9801002-4-2

www.ingramcontent.com/pod-product-compliance
Lightning Source LLC
Chambersburg PA
CBHW032055150426
43194CB00006B/534